PROGRAMMING IN C AND DATA STRUCTURES

SPI PUBLICATIONS

Dr.K.SARASWATHI
Associate Professor
Department of General Engineering
Annai Mathammal Sheela Engineering College
Erumapatty
Tamil Nadu, India

Mrs.R.KALAIVANI
Assistant Professor
Annai Mathammal Sheela College of Education
Erumapatty
Tamil Nadu, India

Mrs.G.LAKSHMIPRIYA
Assistant Professor
PG Department of Computer Applications
Nehru Memorial College
Puthanampatti
Tamil Nadu, India

Mr.P.VELMURUGAN
Computer Instructor (Grade-I)
Government Higher Secondary School
Mallipatinam, Tanjore
Tamil Nadu, India

Published by **SPI Publications**, www.spipublications.in
SPI, the **SPI logo**, and **Split Poetry India** are trademarks of **SPI Publications**, or its affiliates.
ISBN-13: 978-81-990408-3-0

First Edition 2025

SPI Publications

Corporate & Editorial Office

117/2, Sector 37, Khandsa Road,
Gurgaon, Haryana 122 001
Phone: +91 98355 52940
Email: contact@spipublications.in
Website: www.spipublications.in

Processed and Printed in India

PREFACE

The book is meant for Programming in C and Data Structures beginners. We can learn C programming language well with the practice of C programs in that particular programming language and data structure concepts .The purpose of this book is to learn C easily with the variety of programs and data structure concepts. This book makes the reader to get familiar with C and data structure. It mainly focuses on C and data structure concepts.

Unit 1:History of C, Importance of C , Basic structure of C programs , Character set , C Tokens , Keywords and identifiers, Constants , Variables , Data types, Declaration of variables, Assigning values to variables, Defining symbolic constants, Declaring a variable as constant, Input and Output Functions, Operators such as Arithmetic, Relational , Logical , Assignment, Increment, Decrement, Conditional, Bitwise, Special operators, Expressions, Evaluation of expressions , Precedence of Arithmetic operators , Managing I/O operation, Decision Making such as Branching and Looping.

Unit 2: Arrays such as One dimensional array, Declaration, Initialization, Two dimensional array , Declaration, Initialization, User defined Function Definition,Need for user-defined functions, Elements, Return values and their types, Function calls, Function declaration, Category of functions, Nesting of functions, Recursion, Defining a structure, Declaring structure variables, Accessing structure through member, Initialization, Copying and comparing structure variables, Arrays of structures , Unions and Preprocessor.

Unit 3:Understanding pointers, Accessing address of a variable, Declaring pointer variables, Initialization of pointer variables, Accessing a variable through its pointers, Chain of pointers, Pointer expressions, Pointer increment and scalar factor, Pointers and arrays , Defining a file, Opening and closing a file, I/O operations on filesand Error handling.

Unit 4: Introduction to stack, Stacks using dynamic arrays , Queue and Circular Queues using dynamic arrays.

Unit 5: Singly linked lists and chains, Representing chains in C, Introduction to trees, Representation of trees, Introduction to Binary Trees, The Abstract data type, Properties of binary trees, Binary tree representations and Binary Tree Traversal.

ACKNOWLEDGEMENT

We are deeply thankful to Almighty God, whose grace makes all things possible. Without His blessings, none of this would have been achieved.

We extend our heartfelt gratitude to the Management of Annai Mathammal Sheela Engineering College, Erumapatty, for their valuable guidance, unwavering support, and for providing us the opportunity to undertake and complete this book successfully.

We sincerely thank the Management of Annai Mathammal Sheela College of Education, Erumapatty, for their invaluable guidance, constant encouragement, and for granting us the opportunity to carry out and complete this book successfully.

We are equally grateful to the Management of Nehru Memorial College, Puthanampatti, for their continuous encouragement, insightful guidance, and for enabling us to accomplish this endeavor.

We gratefully acknowledge the support of Government Higher Secondary School, Mallipatinam, for providing a nurturing academic environment to carry out and complete this book successfully.

Finally, and most importantly, we thank our beloved family members for their unconditional love, patience, and constant encouragement. Their unwavering support has been a pillar of strength throughout this journey. This book would not have reached completion without them.

Dr.K.SARASWATHI
Mrs.R.KALAIVANI
Mrs.G.LAKSHMIPRIYA
Mr.P. VELMURUGAN

AUTHOR BIOGRAPHIES

Dr. K. Saraswathi M.Sc., M.Phil., M.C.A B.Ed., Ph.D is working as an Associate Professor at Annai Mathammal Sheela Engineering College, Erumapatty.She hasmore than 21 years of teaching and 5 years of research experience. She has published more than 32 research papers in various national and international journals and conferences. A prolific academic author, she has written several textbooks including Problem Solving Using Python Programming, Artificial Intelligence and Machine Learning, Computer Networks, HTML and Office Automation, Advanced Java Programming, Big Data Management and Analytics, and Python Programming. She has also contributed a chapter to the book Advanced Engineering Research and Applications. Dr. K. Saraswathi has actively contributed to faculty development and knowledge dissemination by serving as a resource person for various workshops and seminars at different colleges. Her commitment to continuous professional development is reflected in her participation in 3 seminars, 18 Faculty Development Programs (FDPs), 3 webinars, 2 training programs, and 9 workshops. Her academic dedication and multidisciplinary expertise make her a valuable contributor to the field of engineering education.

Mrs. R. Kalaivani, M.Sc., M.Phil., M.Ed., is currently serving as an Assistant Professor at Annai Mathammal Sheela College of Education, Erumapatty. A passionate and dedicated educator, she brings over 10 years of teaching experience and more than 2 years of research experience to her role. She has successfully guided over 10 students in their academic project work, reflecting her commitment to mentoring and student development. Her area of research expertise includes Cryptography and Network Security, and she has presented her work at a national conference, with one research paper published. She is also actively involved in professional development, having attended 8 Faculty Development Programs (FDPs) and 6 workshops. Her enthusiasm for teaching and her contributions to research make her a valuable asset to the academic community.

Mrs. G. Lakshmipriya holds a Master's degree in Information Technology from Bharathidasan University and an M.Phil. from Kamaraj University. She also qualified the State Eligibility Test (SET) in 2016, conducted by Mother Teresa Women's University. With a solid academic background and a passion for teaching, she brings 17 years of experience in teaching undergraduate students and 10 years of experience in teaching postgraduate students. Over the years, she has guided project work for more than 50 students, reflecting her commitment to academic mentorship. She has published two papers in international journals and one in a national journal. To stay abreast of developments in her field and to enhance her professional skills, she has actively participated in 16 seminars, 2 conferences, and 2 workshops. Her extensive experience and dedication to teaching and research continue to make a significant impact in the academic community.

Mr.P. Velmurugan M.Sc., M.Phil., B.Ed., is a seasoned educator and technology expert with a passion for computer science. Currently serving as a Computer Instructor (Grade-I) at Government Higher Secondary School, Mallipatinam, Tanjore, he has been shaping young minds and fostering a love for technology in his students. Having cleared the State Eligibility Test (SET) and National Eligibility Test (NET), he has demonstrated his expertise and commitment to academic excellence. He has 10+ years of experience as an Assistant Professor, where he honed his teaching skills and developed a deep understanding of computer science concepts. Additionally, he has 1 year of industry experience as a Web Developer. His subject expertise spans mobile app development and web app development, making him a well-rounded authority in the field of computer science.

TABLE OF CONTENTS

UNIT – I

1.1 History of C:

- **Early 1970s**: C was developed by **Dennis Ritchie** at **Bell Labs**. It evolved from the **B language**, which was created by **Ken Thompson**.
- **1972**: C was first implemented on the **UNIX operating system**, helping UNIX become portable across systems.
- **1978**: The **K&R C** version was published in the book "The C Programming Language" by **Kernighan and Ritchie**, becoming the de facto standard.
- **1989**: The first official standard, **ANSI C (C89)**, was released by the American National Standards Institute.
- **1990**: ANSI C became **ISO C (C90)**, an international standard.
- **Later updates**:

  - **C99** (1999): Added features like inline functions, new data types (e.g., long long), and improved support for floating-point arithmetic.
  - **C11** (2011): Introduced multithreading support and improved Unicode handling.
  - **C17** (2017): A bug-fix version of C11.
  - **C23** (2023): Latest revision with new features like enhanced type checking and better support for modern hardware.

1.2 Importance of C:

- **Foundation of many languages**: C has influenced or directly led to the development of C++, Java, Python, and many others.
- **System-level programming**: C is ideal for writing operating systems, drivers, and embedded systems (e.g., Linux is mostly written in C).
- **Portability**: Programs written in C can run on many different machines with little or no modification.
- **Efficiency and speed**: C gives direct access to memory and system resources, allowing for high-performance software.
- **Widely used in education**: It teaches core programming concepts like pointers, memory management, and data structures.

1.3 Basic Structure of a C Program:

```
#include <stdio.h>       // Preprocessor directive
int main()
{           // Main function: Entry point
   printf("Hello!");    // Statement: Function call
   return 0;           // Return statement
```

}

Components

- Preprocessor Directive – #include <stdio.h>: Includes standard input/output functions.
- Main Function – int main(): The starting point of the program.
- Statements – Code inside {} that performs tasks.
- Return Statement – return 0;: Indicates successful execution.

1.4 Character set:

- The **character set in C** includes all valid characters that can be used to write C programs.
- It's divided into several categories

1. Letters

- Uppercase: A to Z
- Lowercase: a to z

2. Digits

- 0 to 9

3. Special Characters

- Symbols like: ~, !, @, #, %, ^, &, *, (,), -, _, +, =, {, }, [,], |, \, :, ;, ", ', <, >, ,, ., ?, /

4. Whitespace Characters

- Space, tab (\t), newline (\n), carriage return (\r), form feed (\f)

5. Escape Sequences

- Special character representations starting with backslash, e.g.:
  - \n (newline)
  - \t (tab)
  - \\ (backslash)
  - \" (double quote)
  - \' (single quote)

These characters are used to form **identifiers, constants, operators, and other syntax elements** in a C program.

1.5 C Tokens:

- **Tokens** are the **smallest elements** of a C program that are meaningful to the compiler.
- C has **6 main types** of tokens

1. **Keywords**
   Reserved words with special meaning (e.g., int, return, if, while).
2. **Identifiers**
   Names for variables, functions, arrays, etc. (e.g., main, sum, x).
3. **Constants**
   Fixed values that don't change (e.g., 10, 3.14, 'A', "Hello").
4. **Operators**
   Symbols that perform operations (e.g., +, -, *, /, =, ==).
5. **Special Symbols**
   Punctuation characters used in syntax (e.g., {}, (), ;, #, []).
6. **Strings**
   A sequence of characters inside double quotes (e.g., "Welcome").

1.6 Keywords and identifiers:

- **Keywords**

Keywords are reserved words that have a predefined meaning in the C++ language. They cannot be used as names for variables, functions, classes, or other identifiers.

Here are some commonly used C++ keywords:

auto	break	case	char	class
const	continue	default	delete	do
double	else	enum	extern	float
for	goto	if	inline	int
long	namespace	new	operator	private
protected	public	register	return	short
signed	sizeof	static	struct	switch
template	this	throw	try	typedef
union	unsigned	using	virtual	void
volatile	while			

- **Identifiers**
    - Identifiers are the names used to identify variables, functions, arrays, classes, etc.
    - They are user-defined and must follow certain rules:

Rules for Identifiers

- Can contain letters (A–Z, a–z), digits (0–9), and underscores (_).
- Must begin with a letter or underscore (not a digit).
- Cannot be a C++ keyword.
- Are case-sensitive (Variable, variable, and VARIABLE are different).

Examples of valid identifiers

- int totalScore;
- float _average;
- char name1;

Examples of invalid identifiers

- int 1stValue; // starts with a digit
- float double; // 'double' is a keyword
- char user-name; // hyphen is not allowed

1.7 Constants:

- **Constants** refer to **fixed values** that do not change during the execution of a program. They can be of various types and are used to make programs more readable and maintainable.

Types of Constants in C

1. **Integer Constants**
    - Whole numbers without a decimal point.
    - Examples: 10, -25, 0

2. **Floating-point Constants**
    - Numbers with a decimal point or in exponential form.
    - Examples: 3.14, -0.001, 2.5e3

3. Character Constants

- A single character enclosed in single quotes.
- Examples: 'A', '9', '#'

4. String Constants

- A sequence of characters enclosed in double quotes.
- Examples: "Hello", "123", "C programming"

5. Enumeration Constants

- Used with enum to assign names to a set of integer values.

```
enum colors { RED, GREEN, BLUE };
```

Declaring Constants

1. **Using #define Preprocessor Directive**

```
#define PI 3.14159
#define MAX 100
```

2. **Using const Keyword**

```
const int max = 100;
const float pi = 3.14;
```

1.8 Variables:

- **Variables** are named memory locations used to store data that can change during program execution.
- **Declaration**: Tells the compiler the variable's name and type.
  - int age;
  - float salary;
  - char grade;
- **Initialization**: Assigns a value at the time of declaration.
  - int age = 25;
- **Naming Rules**:
  - Must start with a letter or underscore.
  - Can contain letters, digits, and underscores.

- Cannot be a keyword (e.g., int, return).
- **Data Types**: Determines the kind of data a variable can hold.
    - int, float, char, double, etc.
- **Scope**: Where the variable is accessible (e.g., global, local).
- **Lifetime**: How long the variable exists during program execution.

1.9 Data Types:

- **Variables** are named memory locations used to store data that can change during program execution.
- **Declaration**: Tells the compiler the variable's name and type.

    - int age;
    - float salary;
    - char grade;

- **Initialization**: Assigns a value at the time of declaration.
    - int age = 25;
- **Naming Rules**:
    - Must start with a letter or underscore.
    - Can contain letters, digits, and underscores.
    - Cannot be a keyword (e.g., int, return).
- **Data Types**: Determines the kind of data a variable can hold.
    - int, float, char, double, etc.
- **Scope**: Where the variable is accessible (e.g., global, local).
- **Lifetime**: How long the variable exists during program execution.
- **Primary Data Types**

Type	Size (Typical)	Description
Int	2 or 4 bytes	Integer numbers
float	4 bytes	Single-precision decimals
double	8 bytes	Double-precision decimals
char	1 byte	Single character

- **Derived Data Types**

    - **Array**: Collection of elements of same type
      int arr[5];
    - **Pointer**: Stores address of another variable
      int *ptr;
    - **Structure (struct)**: Group of variables of different types
    - **Union (union)**: Like structure, but shares memory

- **Function**: Functions returning a specific type

- **Enumeration** (enum)
  - User-defined type with named integer constants

```
enum days { MON, TUE, WED };
```

- **Void**
  - Represents no value; used for functions that return nothing

```
void display();
```

1.10 Declaration of variables:

- **variable declaration** tells the compiler the **name** and **type** of a variable. It **reserves memory** but may or may not assign a value immediately.
- **Syntax**

```
data_type variable_name;
```

Examples

```
int age;        // Declares an integer variable
float price;    // Declares a float variable
char grade;     // Declares a character variable
```

Initialization

```
int age = 25;
float price = 99.99;
char grade = 'A';
```

Multiple Declarations

```
int a, b, c;
float x = 1.1, y = 2.2;
```

Rules for Declaration

- Must be declared before use.
- Cannot use C keywords as variable names.
- Must begin with a letter or underscore.

1.11 Assigning values to variables:

Assigning a value to a variable means **storing a specific value in the memory location** associated with that variable.

Syntax for Assignment

```
variable_name = value;
```

Examples

```
int age;
age = 25;           // Assigns 25 to 'age'

float pi;
pi = 3.14;          // Assigns 3.14 to 'pi'

char grade;
grade = 'A';        // Assigns 'A' to 'grade'
```

Declaration with Assignment (Initialization):

```
int age = 25;
float pi = 3.14;
char grade = 'A';
```

Assigning One Variable to Another:

```
int a = 10;
int b = a;          // Now b is 10
```

1.12 Defining Symbolic constants:

Symbolic constants are defined using the #define preprocessor directive. They represent constant values that **do not change** during program execution and are typically used to make code more readable and maintainable.

Syntax

```
#define NAME value
```

Examples

```
#define PI 3.14159
#define MAX 100
#define NAME "John"
```

- No = sign is used.
- No semicolon ; at the end.
- Replacements are done **before compilation**.

Usage

```
#include <stdio.h>
#define PI 3.14159
int main() {
    float area, radius = 5;
    area = PI * radius * radius;
    printf("Area = %f", area);
    return 0;
}
```

1.13 Declaring a variable as constant:

Declare a variable as **constant** using the const keyword. This means the variable's value **cannot be changed** after initialization.

Syntax:

```
const data_type variable_name = value;
```

Examples:

```
const int max = 100;
const float pi = 3.14;
const char grade = 'A';
```

If you try to modify a const variable later, the compiler will give an **error**:

```
max = 200;  // ✗ Error: assignment of read-only variable
```

1.14 Input and Output Functions:

1. Console I/O Functions

Input Function

- **scanf()**
    - Used to read formatted input from the standard input (keyboard).
    - Syntax: scanf("format_specifier", &variable);
    - **Example:**

```
int a;
scanf("%d", &a);
```

Output Function

- **printf()**
  - Used to print formatted output to the standard output (screen).
  - Syntax: printf("format_specifier", variable);
  - **Example:**

```
int a = 5;
printf("Value: %d", a);
```

2. Character I/O Functions

Input

- **getchar()**
  - Reads a single character from standard input.
  - **Example:**

```
char c = getchar();
```

Output

- **putchar()**
  - Writes a single character to standard output.
  - **Example:**

```
putchar('A');
```

3. String I/O Functions

Input

- **gets()** (deprecated, unsafe)
  - Reads a string until a newline.
  - **Not recommended** due to buffer overflow risk.

- **fgets()**

- Safer alternative to gets().
- Syntax: fgets(str, size, stdin);
- **Example:**

```
char str[50];
fgets(str, 50, stdin);
```

Output

- **puts()**

  - Prints a string followed by a newline.
  - Example:

```
puts("Hello, World!");
```

4. File I/O Functions

Defined in <stdio.h>:

- **fopen(), fclose()** – open and close files
- **fprintf(), fscanf()** – formatted I/O to/from files
- **fgetc(), fputc()** – character I/O from/to files
- **fgets(), fputs()** – string I/O from/to files

1.15 Operators:

Operators are symbols used to perform operations on variables and values. They are grouped based on their functionality:

1. Arithmetic Operators

Used for mathematical operations

Operator	Description	Example
+	Addition	a + b
-	Subtraction	a - b
*	Multiplication	a * b
/	Division	a / b
%	Modulus (remainder)	a % b

2. Relational (Comparison) Operators

Used to compare values

Operator	Description	Example
==	Equal to	a == b
!=	Not equal to	a != b
>	Greater than	a > b
<	Less than	a < b
>=	Greater than or equal	a >= b
<=	Less than or equal	a <= b

3. Logical Operators

Used in logical expressions

Operator	Description	Example
&&	Logical AND	a && b
`		`
!	Logical NOT	!a

4. Assignment Operators

Used to assign values to variables

Operator	Description	Example
=	Assign	a = b
+=	Add and assign	a += b
-=	Subtract and assign	a -= b
*=	Multiply and assign	a *= b
/=	Divide and assign	a /= b
%=	Modulus and assign	a %= b

5. Increment/Decrement Operators

Increase or decrease a variable by 1

Operator	Description	Example
++	Increment	a++ or ++a
--	Decrement	a-- or --a

6. Bitwise Operators

Operate on bits

Operator	Description	Example
&	Bitwise AND	a & b
`	`	Bitwise OR
^	Bitwise XOR	a ^ b
~	Bitwise NOT	~a
<<	Left shift	a << 2
>>	Right shift	a >> 2

7. Conditional (Ternary) Operator

Short-hand for if-else

(condition) ? expression1 : expression2;

Example:

```
int a = 5, b = 10;
int max = (a > b) ? a : b;
```

8. Special Operators

- **sizeof** – Returns size of data type or variable
- **&** – Address-of operator
- ***** – Pointer dereference
- **->** – Access structure member via pointer
- **.** – Access structure member

1.16 Expression and its Evaluation:

1. Constant Expressions

Use only constants and evaluate at compile time.

10 + 5 // evaluates to 15

2. Arithmetic Expressions

Use arithmetic operators to perform calculations.

```
a + b * c - d / e
```

3. Relational Expressions

Compare values using relational operators.

```
a > b    // returns 1 if true, 0 otherwise
```

4. Logical Expressions

Combine multiple conditions using logical operators.

```
(a > b) && (b < c)
```

5. Assignment Expressions

Assign values using the assignment operator =.

```
x = y + 2;
```

6. Increment/Decrement Expressions

Modify a variable's value by 1.

```
x++;  // Post-increment
++x;  // Pre-increment
```

7. Conditional (Ternary) Expression

A compact form of if-else.

```
max = (a > b) ? a : b;
```

8. Function Call Expressions

Calling a function is also an expression.

```
printf("Hello");  // returns number of characters printed
```

Expression Evaluation Example

```
int a = 10, b = 5, c;
c = a + b * 2;  // Evaluates to 10 + (5 * 2) = 20
```

1.17 Precedence of Arithmetic operators:

Arithmetic operator precedence determines the order in which operations are performed in an expression. When multiple operators appear, those with **higher precedence** are evaluated first.

Arithmetic Operator Precedence (from highest to lowest)

Precedence	Operators	Description	Associativity
1 (highest)	*, /, %	Multiplication, Division, Modulus	Left to Right
2	+, -	Addition, Subtraction	Left to Right

Example 1

```
int result = 10 + 5 * 2; // result = 10 + (5 * 2) = 20
```

Because * has higher precedence than +.

Example 2

```
int result = (10 + 5) * 2; // result = 15 * 2 = 30
```

Parentheses override precedence.

Associativity

When two operators have the same precedence, associativity determines the order of evaluation.

For arithmetic operators: **Left to Right**

```
int result = 20 / 5 * 2; // (20 / 5) * 2 = 4 * 2 = 8
```

1.18 Managing I/O operations:

- **Managing I/O operations in C** involves handling input from the user or files and outputting data to the screen or files.
- C provides powerful and flexible I/O through its **Standard I/O Library (<stdio.h>)**.

1. Console I/O (Standard Input/Output)

Input

- scanf() – reads formatted input.

- int x;
- scanf("%d", &x);

- getchar() – reads a single character.
  - char ch = getchar();
- fgets() – reads a line of text (safer for strings).
  - char str[100];
  - fgets(str, 100, stdin);

Output

- printf() – prints formatted output.
  - printf("Value: %d", x);
- putchar() – outputs a single character.
  - putchar('A');
- puts() – prints a string with a newline.
  - puts("Hello");

2. File I/O Operations

- To manage file-based I/O:

Opening Files

- FILE *fp = fopen("file.txt", "r"); // read mode

Reading from File

- char ch = fgetc(fp); // read one character
- fscanf(fp, "%d", &x); // read formatted data
- fgets(str, size, fp); // read string

Writing to File

- fputc('A', fp); // write one character
- fprintf(fp, "%d", x); // formatted write
- fputs("Hello", fp); // write string

Closing Files

- fclose(fp);

3. Error Handling in I/O

Always check for null pointers or errors

```
if (fp == NULL) {
   printf("File could not be opened.\n");
}
```

1.19 Decision Making Statements:

- **Decision-making statements** (also called control statements) allow the program to execute certain code blocks based on conditions.
- These are essential for writing logic-driven programs.

Branching Statements

1. if Statement

Executes a block if the condition is true.

```
if (condition) {
   // statements
}
```

Example1

```
if (a > b) {
   printf("A is greater");
}
```

Example2

```
#include <stdio.h>
int main() {
   int age = 20;
   if (age >= 18) {
      printf("You are eligible to vote.\n");
   }
   return 0;
}
```

2. if...else Statement

Executes one block if true, another if false.

```
if (condition) {
   // true block
```

```
} else {
   // false block
}
```

Example

```
#include <stdio.h>
int main() {
   int num = 5;
   if (num % 2 == 0) {
      printf("Even number\n");
   } else {
      printf("Odd number\n");
   }
   return 0;
}
```

3. else if Ladder

Tests multiple conditions.

```
if (a > b) {
   // Block A
} else if (a < b) {
   // Block B
} else {
   // Block C
}
```

Example

```
#include <stdio.h>
int main() {
   int marks = 85;
   if (marks >= 90) {
      printf("Grade A\n");
   } else if (marks >= 75) {
      printf("Grade B\n");
   } else if (marks >= 60) {
      printf("Grade C\n");
   } else {
      printf("Fail\n");
   }
   return 0;
}
```

4. switch Statement

Selects one of many code blocks based on the value of an expression.

Syntax

```
switch (expression) {
   case value1:
      // statements
      break;
   case value2:
      // statements
      break;
   default:
      // default statements
}
```

Example:

```
#include <stdio.h>
int main() {
   int day = 3;
   switch (day) {
      case 1: printf("Monday\n"); break;
      case 2: printf("Tuesday\n"); break;
      case 3: printf("Wednesday\n"); break;
      default: printf("Invalid day\n");
   }
   return 0;
}
```

5. Conditional (Ternary) Operator

Short form of if...else for expressions.

```
(condition) ? true_value : false_value;
```

Example:

```
#include <stdio.h>
int main() {
   int a = 10, b = 20;
   int max = (a > b) ? a : b;
```

```
    printf("Maximum is %d\n", max);
    return 0;
}
```

Looping Statements

1. for Loop

Used when the number of iterations is known in advance.

Syntax

```
for (initialization; condition; increment/decrement) {
    // code to execute
}
```

Example

Print numbers 1 to 5

```
#include <stdio.h>
int main() {
    for (int i = 1; i <= 5; i++) {
        printf("Number: %d\n", i);
    }
    return 0;
}
```

2. while Loop

Used when the number of iterations is **not known** ahead of time.

Syntax

```
while (condition) {
    // code to execute
}
```

Example:

Print numbers 1 to 5

```
#include <stdio.h>
int main() {
    int i = 1;
    while (i <= 5) {
        printf("Number: %d\n", i);
```

```
    i++;
  }
  return 0;
}
```

3. do...while Loop

Executes the block **at least once**, even if the condition is false.

Syntax

```
do {
  // code to execute
} while (condition);
```

Example

```
#include <stdio.h>
int main() {
  int i = 1;
  do {
    printf("Number: %d\n", i);
    i++;
  } while (i <= 5);
  return 0;
}
```

4. Loop Control Statements

break

Stops the loop immediately.

```
#include <stdio.h>
int main() {
  for (int i = 1; i <= 10; i++) {
    if (i == 6) break;
    printf("%d ", i);
  }
  return 0;
}
```

Output: 1 2 3 4 5

Continue

Skips the current iteration and continues with the next.

```
#include <stdio.h>
int main() {
   for (int i = 1; i <= 5; i++) {
      if (i == 3) continue;
      printf("%d ", i);
   }
   return 0;
}
```

Output: 1 2 4 5

UNIT – II

2.1 Arrays:

An **array** is a collection of elements of the **same data type** stored in **contiguous memory locations**. Arrays are used to store multiple values in a single variable instead of declaring separate variables for each value.

Declaring Arrays

Syntax

```
data_type array_name[size];
```

Example

```
int numbers[5]; // array of 5 integers
```

Initialization

```
int numbers[5] = {10, 20, 30, 40, 50};
```

Accessing Array Elements

Use the **index** (starts from 0):

```
printf("%d", numbers[0]); // prints 10
numbers[2] = 100;         // changes 30 to 100
```

Example: Input and Output of an Integer Array

```
#include <stdio.h>
int main() {
   int i, arr[5];

   // Input
   printf("Enter 5 numbers:\n");
   for (i = 0; i < 5; i++) {
      scanf("%d", &arr[i]);
   }
   // Output
   printf("You entered:\n");
   for (i = 0; i < 5; i++) {
      printf("%d ", arr[i]);
   }
   return 0;
}
```

2.2 One dimensional array:

A **one-dimensional array** in C is a list of elements of the same data type stored in a single row (linearly in memory).

Declaration and Initialization

Syntax

```
data_type array_name[size];                  // Declaration only
data_type array_name[size] = {val1, val2...}; // Declaration with initialization
```

Examples

Example 1: Declare and Assign Later

```
int numbers[5];        // Declaring an array of 5 integers
numbers[0] = 10;
numbers[1] = 20;
numbers[2] = 30;
numbers[3] = 40;
numbers[4] = 50;
```

Example 2: Declare and Initialize Together

```
int numbers[5] = {10, 20, 30, 40, 50};
```

Example 3: Compiler Determines Size Automatically

```
int numbers[] = {10, 20, 30};  // size is 3
```

Example

```
#include <stdio.h>
int main() {
   int numbers[5] = {1, 2, 3, 4, 5};
   for (int i = 0; i < 5; i++) {
      printf("Element %d: %d\n", i, numbers[i]);
   }
   return 0;
}
```

2.3 Two dimensional array:

A **two-dimensional array** in C is like a **table or matrix** with rows and columns. It is declared using two sets of square brackets.

Declaration and Initialization of 2D Arrays

Syntax

```
data_type array_name[rows][columns];
```

Initialization

```
int matrix[2][3] = {
   {1, 2, 3},
   {4, 5, 6}
};
```

This creates a 2x3 matrix:

Initialization Without Specifying Rows:

```
int matrix[][3] = {
   {10, 20, 30},
   {40, 50, 60}
};
```

The compiler infers the number of rows based on the data.

Accessing Elements

```
matrix[0][1]  // refers to element at 1st row, 2nd column → value 2
```

Example: 2D Array Display

```
#include <stdio.h>
int main() {
   int matrix[2][3] = {
      {1, 2, 3},
      {4, 5, 6}
   };

   printf("Matrix elements:\n");
   for (int i = 0; i < 2; i++) {
      for (int j = 0; j < 3; j++) {
         printf("%d ", matrix[i][j]);
      }
      printf("\n");
   }

   return 0;
}
```

2.4 User Defined Functions :

1. Need for User-Defined Functions

- To **break complex problems** into smaller, manageable pieces.
- To **reuse code** without rewriting.
- To improve **readability** and **maintainability** of code.
- To enable **modular programming**.
- To **reduce redundancy** and make debugging easier.

2. Elements of a Function

A typical function in C consists of

- **Function return type**: Type of value the function returns (e.g., int, void).
- **Function name**: Identifier used to call the function.
- **Parameter list (optional)**: Input values the function accepts.
- **Function body**: Block of statements enclosed in {} which performs the task.

3. Function Definition

Defines what the function does.

```
return_type function_name(parameter_list) {
   // function body
   return value;  // if return_type is not void
}
```

Example:

```
int add(int a, int b) {
   return a + b;
}
```

4. Return Values and Their Types

- Functions can return any valid C data type: int, float, char, double, void (if no return).
- Use return statement to send the value back to the caller.
- If the return type is void, no value is returned.

```
void printMessage() {
   printf("Hello\n");
}
```

5. Function Calls

Invoke a function by using its name and passing arguments (if any).

```
int result = add(5, 3);
printf("Sum = %d\n", result);
```

6. Function Declaration (Prototype)

Specifies the function's name, return type, and parameters **before** its use, allowing the compiler to check for errors.

```
int add(int, int);  // function prototype
```

This helps when the function is defined after main() or in another file.

7. Categories of Functions

a) Library Functions

- Predefined functions provided by C Standard Library (e.g., printf(), scanf(), strlen()).

b) User-Defined Functions

- Functions written by the programmer.

c) Based on Parameters and Return Types

Type	Description	Example
No parameters, no return	Performs task, returns nothing	void greet()
Parameters, no return	Takes inputs, returns nothing	void printSum(int a, int b)
No parameters, return	Returns a value, no inputs	int getRandomNumber()
Parameters and return	Takes inputs and returns value	int add(int a, int b)

1. No Parameters, No Return Value

- The function neither accepts any input nor returns any output.
- Typically used for tasks like displaying messages.

Example

```
#include <stdio.h>
void greet() {
   printf("Hello! Welcome to C programming.\n");
}
```

```
int main() {
    greet();  // Calling the function
    return 0;
}
```

2. Parameters but No Return Value

- The function takes input parameters but does not return a value.
- Useful when the function performs an action but doesn't compute a result.

Example

```
#include <stdio.h>
void printSum(int a, int b) {
    int sum = a + b;
    printf("Sum = %d\n", sum);
}
int main() {
    printSum(10, 20);  // Output: Sum = 30
    return 0;
}
```

3. No Parameters but Return Value

- The function does not take any input but returns a value.
- Used when a fixed or computed result needs to be returned.

Example

```
#include <stdio.h>
int getRandomNumber() {
    return 42;  // Fixed number for example
}
int main() {
    int num = getRandomNumber();
    printf("Random Number: %d\n", num);
    return 0;
}
```

4. Parameters and Return Value

- The function accepts input parameters and returns a result.
- This is the most common type, e.g., arithmetic operations.

Example

```
#include <stdio.h>
```

```c
int multiply(int x, int y) {
    return x * y;
}
int main() {
    int result = multiply(5, 4);
    printf("Product = %d\n", result);  // Output: Product = 20
    return 0;
}
```

8. Nesting of Functions

- Calling a function **from within another function**.
- **Example**

```c
int square(int x) {
    return x * x;
}
int sumOfSquares(int a, int b) {
    return square(a) + square(b);
}
int main() {
    printf("%d\n", sumOfSquares(3, 4)); // Output: 25
    return 0;
}
```

9. Recursion in C

- A function that **calls itself** directly or indirectly.
- Used for problems that can be divided into smaller similar subproblems.
- Must have a **base case** to stop recursion, otherwise it leads to infinite recursion.

Example: Factorial using recursion

```c
int factorial(int n) {
    if (n == 0)        // base case
        return 1;
    else
        return n * factorial(n - 1);  // recursive call
}
int main() {
    int num = 5;
    printf("Factorial of %d is %d\n", num, factorial(num));
    return 0;
}
```

2.5 Structures:

A **structure** is a user-defined data type that groups variables of different types under a single name.

1. Defining a Structure

Use the keyword struct to define a structure.

```
struct Person {
   char name[50];
   int age;
   float salary;
};
```

This defines a structure named Person with three members: name, age, and salary.

2. Declaring Structure Variables

After defining a structure, declare variables of that type.

```
struct Person p1, p2;
```

Define and declare at the same time:

```
struct Person {
   char name[50];
   int age;
   float salary;
} p1, p2;
```

3. Accessing Structure Members

Use the dot . operator to access members of a structure variable.

```
p1.age = 25;
strcpy(p1.name, "Alice");
p1.salary = 50000.0;
```

4. Initialization of Structure Variables

You can initialize a structure at declaration:

```
struct Person p1 = {"Bob", 30, 60000.0};
```

5. Copying Structure Variables

You can assign one structure variable to another directly:

```
p2 = p1;  // copies all members from p1 to p2
```

6. Comparing Structure Variables

C does **not** support direct comparison of structures using ==. You need to compare each member manually:

Example

```
int areEqual = 0;
if (strcmp(p1.name, p2.name) == 0 && p1.age == p2.age && p1.salary == p2.salary) {
    areEqual = 1;
}
```

7. Arrays of Structures

You can create an array to store multiple structures:

```
struct Person employees[3];
```

Example: Input and display array of structures

```
#include <stdio.h>
#include <string.h>
struct Person {
    char name[50];
    int age;
    float salary;
};
int main() {
    struct Person employees[3];
    // Input details
    for(int i = 0; i < 3; i++) {
        printf("Enter details for employee %d:\n", i+1);
        printf("Name: ");
        scanf("%s", employees[i].name);
        printf("Age: ");
        scanf("%d", &employees[i].age);
        printf("Salary: ");
        scanf("%f", &employees[i].salary);
    }
// Display details
```

```
    printf("\nEmployee Details:\n");
    for(int i = 0; i < 3; i++) {
        printf("Employee %d: %s, Age: %d, Salary: %.2f\n",
            i+1, employees[i].name, employees[i].age, employees[i].salary);
    }
    return 0;
}
```

2.6 Unions:

- A **union** is a special data type in C that allows storing **different data types in the same memory location**.
- Unlike structures, **all members of a union share the same memory space**.
- The size of the union is equal to the size of its largest member.
- Only **one member can contain a value at a time**.

1. Unions use

- To save memory when you need to store **different types of data but never at the same time**.
- Useful in applications like **interpreting the same data in different formats** (e.g., hardware interfacing, protocol parsing).

2. Defining a Union

```
union Data {
    int i;
    float f;
    char str[20];
};
```

Here, Data can store either an int, a float, or a string of characters, but only one at a time.

3. Declaring Union Variables

```
union Data data;
```

4. Accessing Union Members

Use the **dot operator** just like with structures

```
data.i = 10;
printf("data.i = %d\n", data.i);
```

```
data.f = 220.5;
printf("data.f = %.2f\n", data.f);

strcpy(data.str, "Hello");
printf("data.str = %s\n", data.str);
```

Since all members share the same memory

- Writing to one member **overwrites** the previous value.
- Reading a member different from the last written may produce unexpected results.

Example

```
#include <stdio.h>
#include <string.h>
union Data {
    int i;
    float f;
    char str[20];
};
int main() {
    union Data data;
    data.i = 10;
    printf("data.i = %d\n", data.i);
    data.f = 220.5;
    printf("data.f = %.2f\n", data.f);
    strcpy(data.str, "Hello, World!");
    printf("data.str = %s\n", data.str);
    // Now printing all members again to see what happens
    printf("After assigning str:\n");
    printf("data.i = %d\n", data.i);    // May print garbage
    printf("data.f = %.2f\n", data.f);  // May print garbage
    printf("data.str = %s\n", data.str);
    return 0;
}
```

Explanation

- When data.i is assigned, you get the correct integer.
- Assigning data.f overwrites the memory, so data.i's previous value is lost.
- Assigning data.str overwrites the memory again.
- Accessing any other member than the last assigned one results in unpredictable data.

2.7 Preprocessor:

- The **C Preprocessor** is a **program that processes your source code before compilation**.
- It handles directives that begin with #, such as #include, #define, #ifdef, etc.
- The preprocessor performs **text substitution, macro expansion, file inclusion**, and conditional compilation.
- It helps make your program more flexible, portable, and easier to maintain.

Common Preprocessor Directives

Directive	Purpose
#include	Include the contents of another file
#define	Define a macro (constant or function-like)
#undef	Undefine a macro
#ifdef / #ifndef	Conditional compilation based on whether a macro is defined
#if / #elif / #else / #endif	Conditional compilation based on expressions
#error	Generate a compilation error with a message
#pragma	Special compiler instructions (varies by compiler)

1. #include

Includes another file's content in your source code. Used to include standard libraries or user-defined headers.

```
#include <stdio.h>   // Standard library
#include "myheader.h" // User-defined file
```

2. #define

Defines constants or macros.

a) Constant Macro

```
#define PI 3.14159
```

Usage

```
float area = PI * r * r;
```

b) Function-like Macro

```
#define SQUARE(x) ((x) * (x))
```

Usage

```
int y = SQUARE(5);  // y = 25
```

3. Conditional Compilation

You can include or exclude parts of code based on macros.

```
#define DEBUG
#ifdef DEBUG
 printf("Debug mode enabled\n");
#endif
```

4. #undef

Used to undefine a macro:

```
#undef PI
```

Example: Using Preprocessor Directives

```
#include <stdio.h>
#define MAX 100
#define SQUARE(x) ((x) * (x))
int main() {
   int a = 5, b = 10;
   int max_val = MAX;
   printf("Square of %d is %d\n", a, SQUARE(a));
   printf("Max value is %d\n", max_val);
   #ifdef DEBUG
      printf("Debugging is enabled.\n");
   #else
      printf("Debugging is disabled.\n");
   #endif
   return 0;
}
```

Works

- The preprocessor replaces MAX with 100.
- SQUARE(a) is replaced by ((a) * (a)).
- If DEBUG is defined, the debug message is printed, otherwise not.

UNIT- III

3.1 Understanding Pointers:

- A **pointer** is a variable that stores the **memory address of another variable**.
- Pointers allow **dynamic memory access**, **efficient array handling**, and are crucial for working with functions and data structures like linked lists.

3.2 Accessing Address of a Variable (& operator):

```
int a = 10;
printf("Address of a: %p\n", &a);
```

&a gives the **address** of variable a.

3.3 Declaring Pointer Variables:

```
int *ptr; // pointer to int
char *cptr; // pointer to char
float *fptr; // pointer to float
```

3.4 Initialization of Pointer Variables:

```
int a = 20;
int *ptr = &a;
```

ptr now holds the address of a.

3.5 Accessing a Variable Through Its Pointer (* operator):

```
printf("Value of a: %d\n", *ptr);  // dereferencing
```

*ptr gives the **value stored at the address** in ptr.

3.6 Chain of Pointers (Pointer to Pointer):

```
int a = 10;
int *p = &a;
int **pp = &p;
printf("Value of a: %d\n", **pp);  // Double dereference
```

This is a **pointer to a pointer**. Useful for multidimensional arrays, dynamic memory, etc.

3.7 Pointer Expressions:

Pointers support arithmetic like addition and subtraction based on the data type size:

```c
int arr[] = {10, 20, 30};
int *p = arr;

printf("%d\n", *(p + 1)); // Outputs 20
```

This moves the pointer to the next integer (4 bytes ahead on most systems).

3.8 Pointer Increment and Scalar Factor:

Pointer arithmetic is scaled by the size of the data type:

```c
int a[3] = {1, 2, 3};
int *p = a;
printf("%p\n", p);       // Original address
p++;                     // Moves 4 bytes ahead (for int)
printf("%p\n", p);       // New address
```

The pointer automatically advances by the size of the type it points to.

3.9 Pointers and Arrays:

Arrays and pointers are closely related.

```c
int arr[3] = {10, 20, 30};
int *p = arr;

for (int i = 0; i < 3; i++) {
   printf("%d ", *(p + i));  // Same as arr[i]
}
```

You can treat a pointer like an array name and vice versa.

Example:

```c
#include <stdio.h>
int main() {
   int a = 5;
   int *p = &a;
   int **pp = &p;
   printf("Value of a: %d\n", a);
   printf("Address of a: %p\n", &a);
   printf("Value using pointer: %d\n", *p);
   printf("Address stored in pointer: %p\n", p);
```

```
    printf("Value using pointer to pointer: %d\n", **pp);
    // Pointer and Array
    int arr[] = {1, 2, 3};
    int *ptr = arr;
    printf("\nArray elements using pointer:\n");
    for (int i = 0; i < 3; i++) {
        printf("%d ", *(ptr + i));  // same as arr[i]
    }
    return 0;
}
```

3.10 File Management:

Files are used to **store data permanently**. You can perform operations such as read, write, append, etc., using the **file I/O functions** provided by the standard library (<stdio.h>).

1. Defining a File Pointer

Before working with files, define a **FILE pointer**:

```
FILE *fp;
```

2. Opening a File

Use the fopen() function:

```
fp = fopen("filename.txt", "mode");
```

Common Modes

Mode	Description
"r"	Open for reading (file must exist)
"w"	Open for writing (creates new or erases existing)
"a"	Open for appending
"r+"	Read and write
"w+"	Write and read
"a+"	Append and read

3. Closing a File

Always close a file to free resources:

```
fclose(fp);
```

4. I/O Operations on Files

a) Writing to a File

```
FILE *fp = fopen("output.txt", "w");
fprintf(fp, "Hello, file!\n");
fputs("Another line\n", fp);
fclose(fp);
```

b) Reading from a File

```
FILE *fp = fopen("output.txt", "r");
char str[100];
fgets(str, 100, fp);        // Reads one line
fscanf(fp, "%s", str);      // Reads one word
fclose(fp);
```

5. Error Handling in File I/O

Always check if the file is successfully opened:

```
FILE *fp = fopen("data.txt", "r");
if (fp == NULL) {
   perror("Error opening file");
   return 1;
}
```

- perror() gives a system-defined error message.
- You can also use feof() and ferror().

Example: Reading and Writing With Error Checking

```
#include <stdio.h>
int main() {
   FILE *fp;
   // Writing to file
   fp = fopen("sample.txt", "w");
   if (fp == NULL) {
      perror("Error opening file for writing");
      return 1;
   }
   fprintf(fp, "This is a test file.\n");
   fputs("Second line of text.\n", fp);
   fclose(fp);
   // Reading from file
```

```
    fp = fopen("sample.txt", "r");
    if (fp == NULL) {
        perror("Error opening file for reading");
        return 1;
    }
    char ch;
    printf("Contents of file:\n");
    while ((ch = fgetc(fp)) != EOF) {
        putchar(ch);
    }
    fclose(fp);
    return 0;
}
```

Function	Purpose
fopen()	Opens a file
fclose()	Closes a file
fprintf()	Writes formatted data to a file
fscanf()	Reads formatted data from a file
fgets()	Reads a line from file
fputs()	Writes a string to file
fgetc()	Reads a character from file
feof()	Checks for end-of-file
ferror()	Checks for file error
perror()	Prints error message

UNIT – IV

4.1 Stack:

A **stack** is a **linear data structure** that follows the **LIFO** principle.

Last In, First Out

- This means the **last element** inserted (pushed) into the stack will be the **first** one to be removed (popped).

- Think of a **stack of plates**: you add a plate on top, and you remove the topmost plate first.

Basic Structure

A stack consists of

- An array (or linked list) to store elements
- A pointer/index to the **top** of the stack
- A maximum size (if using arrays)

4.2 Stack Operations:

Operation	Description
push(x)	Inserts element x onto the top
pop()	Removes and returns the top element
peek() or top()	Returns the top element without removing it
isEmpty()	Returns true if the stack is empty
isFull()	(Array stack) Checks if stack is full (optional in dynamic stack)

4.3 Types of Stack Implementation:

1. Static Stack (using arrays)

- Fixed size
- Easy to implement
- Limited by predefined capacity

2. Dynamic Stack (using linked list or dynamic arrays)

- Grows as needed
- Efficient use of memory

Example (Array-based)

Imagine pushing 10, 20, 30:

Initial Stack: []
After push(10): [10]

After push(20): [10, 20]
After push(30): [10, 20, 30]

Now pop() will return 30, and the stack becomes [10, 20].

4.4 Applications of Stack:

Area	Example
Programming	Function call stack, recursion handling
Compilers	Syntax parsing, expression evaluation
OS	Undo operations, backtracking
Web	Browser history
Data Structures	Used in DFS traversal, reversing data

Stack in Real Life

- Plates in a stack
- Pile of books
- Undo feature in text editors
- Backtracking in puzzles (like Sudoku or maze solving)

4.5 Stacks using dynamic arrays:

A **stack** is a linear data structure that follows **LIFO (Last In, First Out)** principle.

The operations typically supported are

- push() – Insert an element.
- pop() – Remove the top element.
- peek() – View the top element.
- isEmpty() – Check if the stack is empty.

When using **dynamic arrays**, the array grows as needed using realloc().

C Implementation

```
#include <stdio.h>
#include <stdlib.h>

typedef struct Stack {
    int *arr;       // Dynamic array to hold elements
    int top;        // Index of top element
```

```
    int capacity;   // Current capacity of the stack
} Stack;

// Function to initialize the stack
void initStack(Stack *stack, int capacity) {
    stack->capacity = capacity;
    stack->top = -1;
    stack->arr = (int *)malloc(capacity * sizeof(int));
}

// Function to check if the stack is empty
int isEmpty(Stack *stack) {
    return stack->top == -1;
}

// Function to resize the stack (double the capacity)
void resize(Stack *stack) {
    stack->capacity *= 2;
    stack->arr = (int *)realloc(stack->arr, stack->capacity * sizeof(int));
}

// Function to push an element onto the stack
void push(Stack *stack, int value) {
    if (stack->top == stack->capacity - 1) {
        resize(stack); // Resize if full
    }
    stack->arr[++stack->top] = value;
    printf("Pushed %d\n", value);
}

// Function to pop an element from the stack
int pop(Stack *stack) {
    if (isEmpty(stack)) {
        printf("Stack Underflow\n");
        return -1;
    }
    return stack->arr[stack->top--];
}

// Function to peek at the top element
```

```
int peek(Stack *stack) {
    if (isEmpty(stack)) {
        printf("Stack is empty\n");
        return -1;
    }
    return stack->arr[stack->top];
}

// Function to free stack memory
void freeStack(Stack *stack) {
    free(stack->arr);
}

int main() {
    Stack s;
    initStack(&s, 2); // Start with capacity 2

    push(&s, 10);
    push(&s, 20);
    push(&s, 30);  // Should trigger resize

    printf("Top element is: %d\n", peek(&s));
    printf("Popped element: %d\n", pop(&s));
    printf("Popped element: %d\n", pop(&s));
    printf("Popped element: %d\n", pop(&s));
    printf("Popped element: %d\n", pop(&s)); // Should show underflow

    freeStack(&s);
    return 0;
}
```

Output

```
Pushed 10
Pushed 20
Pushed 30
Top element is: 30
Popped element: 30
Popped element: 20
Popped element: 10
Stack Underflow
```

Popped element: -1

4.6 Queue:

A **queue** is a **linear data structure** that follows the **FIFO** principle.

First In, First Out

- This means the **first element** inserted into the queue will be the **first one** to be removed.
- Think of a **line at a ticket counter**—the first person in line is served first.

Basic Structure of a Queue

A queue usually has

- A front pointer (where elements are dequeued)
- A rear pointer (where elements are enqueued)
- A container like an array or linked list to store data

4.7 Basic Queue Operations:

Operation	Description
enqueue(x)	Inserts element x at the rear
dequeue()	Removes and returns the element from the front
peek() or front()	Returns the front element without removing it
isEmpty()	Checks if the queue is empty
isFull()	(Only for static queues) Checks if queue is full

4.8 Types of Queue Implementation:

1. Static Queue (Array-based)

- Fixed size
- Can waste space unless circular

2. Dynamic Queue (Using Dynamic Array or Linked List)

- Resizable
- Efficient for growing datasets

3. Circular Queue

- Overcomes the limitation of wasted space in static arrays

4.9 Applications of Queues:

Area	Example
OS	CPU scheduling, I/O buffering
Networking	Data packet management
Simulations	Order processing, printing queue
BFS Algorithm	Level order traversal in trees/graphs

4.10 C Implementation Using Dynamic Arrays:

```
#include <stdio.h>
#include <stdlib.h>

typedef struct Queue {
   int *arr;
   int front, rear, size, capacity;
} Queue;

// Initialize the queue
void initQueue(Queue *q, int capacity) {
   q->capacity = capacity;
   q->front = q->size = 0;
   q->rear = capacity - 1;
   q->arr = (int*)malloc(capacity * sizeof(int));
}

// Check if the queue is full
int isFull(Queue *q) {
   return q->size == q->capacity;
}

// Check if the queue is empty
int isEmpty(Queue *q) {
   return q->size == 0;
}

// Resize the queue if needed
void resize(Queue *q) {
```

```
    q->capacity *= 2;
    q->arr = (int*)realloc(q->arr, q->capacity * sizeof(int));
}

// Enqueue an element
void enqueue(Queue *q, int value) {
    if (isFull(q)) {
        resize(q);
    }
    q->rear = (q->rear + 1) % q->capacity;
    q->arr[q->rear] = value;
    q->size++;
    printf("Enqueued: %d\n", value);
}

// Dequeue an element
int dequeue(Queue *q) {
    if (isEmpty(q)) {
        printf("Queue Underflow\n");
        return -1;
    }
    int item = q->arr[q->front];
    q->front = (q->front + 1) % q->capacity;
    q->size--;
    return item;
}

// Peek at front element
int front(Queue *q) {
    if (isEmpty(q)) return -1;
    return q->arr[q->front];
}

// Free the queue
void freeQueue(Queue *q) {
    free(q->arr);
}

int main() {
    Queue q;
```

```
    initQueue(&q, 2);

    enqueue(&q, 10);
    enqueue(&q, 20);
    enqueue(&q, 30); // triggers resize
    printf("Front: %d\n", front(&q));
    printf("Dequeued: %d\n", dequeue(&q));
    printf("Dequeued: %d\n", dequeue(&q));
    printf("Dequeued: %d\n", dequeue(&q));
    printf("Dequeued: %d\n", dequeue(&q)); // underflow
    freeQueue(&q);
    return 0;
}
```

Output

```
Enqueued: 10
Enqueued: 20
Enqueued: 30
Front: 10
Dequeued: 10
Dequeued: 20
Dequeued: 30
Queue Underflow
Dequeued: -1
```

4.11 Circular queues using dynamic arrays:

A **Circular Queue** is a linear data structure that uses a **circular arrangement** of storage to make full use of the array.

It follows **FIFO (First-In, First-Out)** like a normal queue, but

- The **rear** wraps around to the front if there's space.
- No need to shift elements after dequeue.

This avoids wasted space from simple array-based queues.

Circular Queues use

In a normal queue:

- After multiple dequeues, front moves forward.
- But space behind front isn't reused.

In a **circular queue**:

- When rear reaches the end, it wraps to the start (if space is available).

4.12 Operations in Circular Queue:

Operation	**Description**
enqueue(x)	Add element at rear
dequeue()	Remove element from front
isFull()	Check if queue is full
isEmpty()	Check if queue is empty
front()	View front element
resize()	Expand array size dynamically

4.13 C Implementation Using Dynamic Arrays:

```
#include <stdio.h>
#include <stdlib.h>

typedef struct CircularQueue {
    int *arr;
    int front, rear, size, capacity;
} CircularQueue;

// Initialize the queue
void initQueue(CircularQueue *q, int capacity) {
    q->capacity = capacity;
    q->arr = (int *)malloc(capacity * sizeof(int));
    q->front = 0;
    q->rear = -1;
    q->size = 0;
}

// Check if queue is empty
int isEmpty(CircularQueue *q) {
    return q->size == 0;
}

// Check if queue is full
int isFull(CircularQueue *q) {
    return q->size == q->capacity;
}
```

```
// Resize the queue
void resizeQueue(CircularQueue *q) {
    int newCapacity = q->capacity * 2;
    int *newArr = (int *)malloc(newCapacity * sizeof(int));

    for (int i = 0; i < q->size; i++) {
        newArr[i] = q->arr[(q->front + i) % q->capacity];
    }

    free(q->arr);
    q->arr = newArr;
    q->capacity = newCapacity;
    q->front = 0;
    q->rear = q->size - 1;
}

// Enqueue an element
void enqueue(CircularQueue *q, int value) {
    if (isFull(q)) {
        resizeQueue(q);
    }
    q->rear = (q->rear + 1) % q->capacity;
    q->arr[q->rear] = value;
    q->size++;
    printf("Enqueued: %d\n", value);
}

// Dequeue an element
int dequeue(CircularQueue *q) {
    if (isEmpty(q)) {
        printf("Queue Underflow\n");
        return -1;
    }
    int data = q->arr[q->front];
    q->front = (q->front + 1) % q->capacity;
    q->size--;
    return data;
}
```

```
// Peek front element
int getFront(CircularQueue *q) {
    if (isEmpty(q)) return -1;
    return q->arr[q->front];
}

// Free the queue
void freeQueue(CircularQueue *q) {
    free(q->arr);
}

int main() {
    CircularQueue q;
    initQueue(&q, 3);

    enqueue(&q, 10);
    enqueue(&q, 20);
    enqueue(&q, 30);

    printf("Front: %d\n", getFront(&q));

    enqueue(&q, 40); // triggers resize

    printf("Dequeued: %d\n", dequeue(&q));
    printf("Dequeued: %d\n", dequeue(&q));

    enqueue(&q, 50);
    enqueue(&q, 60);

    printf("Front: %d\n", getFront(&q));

    freeQueue(&q);
    return 0;
}
```

Output

Enqueued: 10
Enqueued: 20
Enqueued: 30
Front: 10
Enqueued: 40

Dequeued: 10
Dequeued: 20
Enqueued: 50
Enqueued: 60
Front: 30

UNIT- V

5.1 Singly Linked List:

A **singly linked list** is a **linear data structure** where each element (called a **node**) contains:

1. **Data**
2. A **pointer** to the next node

Unlike arrays, linked lists don't store elements in contiguous memory locations. Instead, each node points to the next.

Structure of a Node

In C

```
struct Node {
    int data;           // Value of the node
    struct Node *next;  // Pointer to the next node
};
```

- data stores the actual value.
- next stores the address of the next node.
- The **last node's next pointer** is NULL, indicating the end of the list.

5.2 Chain:

A **chain** is just another way to refer to a **linked list** — it's a "chain" of nodes linked by pointers.

Example

- Define a node structure (the basic unit of a chain)
- Create several nodes
- Link them together to form a chain
- Traverse and display the chain

Example: Representing a Chain in C

```
#include <stdio.h>
#include <stdlib.h>
// Define the structure for a node (each link in the chain)
struct Node {
    int data;
```

```
    struct Node* next;
};
int main() {
    // Create individual nodes
    struct Node* node1 = (struct Node*)malloc(sizeof(struct Node));
    struct Node* node2 = (struct Node*)malloc(sizeof(struct Node));
    struct Node* node3 = (struct Node*)malloc(sizeof(struct Node));
    // Assign data to nodes
    node1->data = 10;
    node2->data = 20;
    node3->data = 30;
    // Link the nodes to form a chain
    node1->next = node2;
    node2->next = node3;
    node3->next = NULL; // End of the chain
    // Head points to the start of the chain
    struct Node* head = node1;
    // Traverse and print the chain
    printf("Chain (Linked List): ");
    struct Node* current = head;
    while (current != NULL) {
        printf("%d -> ", current->data);
        current = current->next;
    }
    printf("NULL\n");
    // Free allocated memory
    free(node1);
    free(node2);
    free(node3);
    return 0;
}
```

Output

Chain (Linked List): 10 -> 20 -> 30 -> NULL

5.3 Representation of a Singly Linked List in C:

```
#include <stdio.h>
#include <stdlib.h>
// Define a node
struct Node {
    int data;
```

```
    struct Node* next;
};
// Function to create a new node
struct Node* createNode(int value) {
    struct Node* newNode = (struct Node*)malloc(sizeof(struct Node));
    newNode->data = value;
    newNode->next = NULL;
    return newNode;
}
// Function to insert at the end
void insertEnd(struct Node** head, int value) {
    struct Node* newNode = createNode(value);
    if (*head == NULL) {
        *head = newNode;
        return;
    }
    struct Node* temp = *head;
    while (temp->next != NULL)
        temp = temp->next;
    temp->next = newNode;
}
// Function to display the list
void displayList(struct Node* head) {
    struct Node* current = head;
    printf("Linked List: ");
    while (current != NULL) {
        printf("%d -> ", current->data);
        current = current->next;
    }
    printf("NULL\n");
}

// Function to free the list
void freeList(struct Node* head) {
    struct Node* temp;
    while (head != NULL) {
        temp = head;
        head = head->next;
        free(temp);
    }
```

```
}
int main() {
    struct Node* head = NULL;
    insertEnd(&head, 10);
    insertEnd(&head, 20);
    insertEnd(&head, 30);
    displayList(head);
    freeList(head);
    return 0;
}
```

Output

Linked List: 10 -> 20 -> 30 -> NULL

Explanation

- **Dynamic memory** is used (malloc) to allocate nodes at runtime.
- We use a **pointer to pointer (Node**)** in insertEnd to modify the original head.
- NULL is used to mark the end of the chain.
- You can traverse the list using a while loop until the next pointer is NULL.

5.4 Real-World Applications:

- Managing dynamic data (e.g., playlists, task queues)
- Implementing stacks and queues
- Memory management (garbage collection)
- Symbol tables in compilers

5.5 Tree:

A **tree** is a **non-linear hierarchical data structure** consisting of **nodes** connected by **edges**.

KeyFeatures

- One node is designated as the **root**.
- Each node may have **zero or more children**.
- There is exactly **one path** between any two nodes.

Basic Terminology

Term	Meaning
Root	Top-most node
Child	Node connected below another node

Term	Meaning
Parent	Node connected above a node
Leaf	Node with no children
Subtree	Tree formed from a child node
Depth	Distance from root to the node
Height	Longest path from node to leaf

5.6 Tree Representation in C:

There are two common ways to represent trees:

1. Using Nodes and Pointers (Dynamic / Linked Representation)

Each node contains

- Data
- Pointers to its children

2. Using Arrays (Static Representation)

- Mostly used for **binary heaps** or **complete binary trees**.

5.7 C Implementation of a Simple Binary Tree:

- Define a tree node
- Create nodes
- Link them to form a binary tree
- Traverse the tree (preorder, inorder, postorder)

Example

```
#include <stdio.h>

#include <stdlib.h>

// Node definition

struct Node {

    int data;
```

```
    struct Node* left;
    struct Node* right;
};
// Create a new node
struct Node* createNode(int value) {
    struct Node* newNode = (struct Node*)malloc(sizeof(struct Node));
    if (newNode == NULL) {
        printf("Memory allocation failed\n");
        exit(1);
    }
    newNode->data = value;
    newNode->left = NULL;
    newNode->right = NULL;
    return newNode;
}
// Inorder traversal
void inorder(struct Node* root) {
    if (root != NULL) {
        inorder(root->left);
        printf("%d ", root->data);
        inorder(root->right);
    }
```

```
}
// Preorder traversal
void preorder(struct Node* root) {
    if (root != NULL) {
        printf("%d ", root->data);
        preorder(root->left);
        preorder(root->right);
    }
}
// Postorder traversal
void postorder(struct Node* root) {
    if (root != NULL) {
        postorder(root->left);
        postorder(root->right);
        printf("%d ", root->data);
    }
}


int main() {
    // Create the tree manually
    /*
          10
```

```
    / \
   6   15
  /    / \
 3    12  18
*/
struct Node* root = createNode(10);
root->left = createNode(6);
root->right = createNode(15);
root->left->left = createNode(3);
root->right->left = createNode(12);
root->right->right = createNode(18);
// Print tree traversals
printf("Inorder Traversal: ");
inorder(root);
printf("\n");
printf("Preorder Traversal: ");
preorder(root);
printf("\n");
printf("Postorder Traversal: ");
postorder(root);
printf("\n");
return 0;
```

```
}
```

Output

Inorder Traversal: 3 6 10 12 15 18

Preorder Traversal: 10 6 3 15 12 18

Postorder Traversal: 3 6 12 18 15 10

5.8 Binary Tree:

A **Binary Tree** is a hierarchical data structure in which each node has **at most two children**, called:

- **Left child**
- **Right child**

Abstract Data Type (ADT)

A **binary tree ADT** defines:

- A **collection of nodes**
- A node has:
    - data
    - left pointer
    - right pointer

Operations

- Create, insert, delete, traverse, search, etc.

Properties of Binary Trees

Let n be the number of nodes and h be the height of the tree:

Property	Description
Max nodes at level l	2^l

Property	Description
Max nodes in tree of height h	2^(h+1) - 1
Min possible height (with n nodes)	ceil(log2(n+1)) - 1
Max height (degenerate tree)	n - 1

Types

- **Full Binary Tree**: Every node has 0 or 2 children
- **Perfect Binary Tree**: Full and all leaves at same level
- **Complete Binary Tree**: All levels full except maybe last
- **Skewed Tree**: All nodes only have left or right child

5.9 Representation of Binary Trees in C:

Using Structures and Pointers (Dynamic Representation)

```
struct Node {
   int data;
   struct Node* left;
   struct Node* right;
};
```

This allows:

- Recursively linking nodes
- Easy traversal and modification

5.10 Binary Tree Traversals:

1. Inorder (Left, Root, Right)
2. Preorder (Root, Left, Right)
3. Postorder (Left, Right, Root)

C Implementation

```
#include <stdio.h>
#include <stdlib.h>

// Node structure
struct Node {
   int data;
   struct Node* left;
   struct Node* right;
};
```

```
// Function to create a new node
struct Node* createNode(int value) {
    struct Node* newNode = (struct Node*)malloc(sizeof(struct Node));
    newNode->data = value;
    newNode->left = NULL;
    newNode->right = NULL;
    return newNode;
}
// Inorder Traversal: Left -> Root -> Right
void inorder(struct Node* root) {
    if (root != NULL) {
        inorder(root->left);
        printf("%d ", root->data);
        inorder(root->right);
    }
}
// Preorder Traversal: Root -> Left -> Right
void preorder(struct Node* root) {
    if (root != NULL) {
        printf("%d ", root->data);
        preorder(root->left);
        preorder(root->right);
    }
}
// Postorder Traversal: Left -> Right -> Root
void postorder(struct Node* root) {
    if (root != NULL) {
        postorder(root->left);
        postorder(root->right);
        printf("%d ", root->data);
    }
}
int main() {
    // Manually build a binary tree
    /*
          1
         / \
        2   3
       / \
```

```
  4  5
*/
struct Node* root = createNode(1);
root->left = createNode(2);
root->right = createNode(3);
root->left->left = createNode(4);
root->left->right = createNode(5);
// Traversals
printf("Inorder Traversal: ");
inorder(root);
printf("\n");
printf("Preorder Traversal: ");
preorder(root);
printf("\n");
printf("Postorder Traversal: ");
postorder(root);
printf("\n");
return 0;
}
```

Output

Inorder Traversal: 4 2 5 1 3
Preorder Traversal: 1 2 4 5 3
Postorder Traversal: 4 5 2 3 1